FABULOUS FLORALS
COLORING BOOK

ARROLYNN WEIDERHOLD

DESIGN ORIGINALS
an Imprint of Fox Chapel Publishing
www.d-originals.com

It's Time to Start Coloring!

We're so glad you've picked up this coloring book, because we know you're going to find exactly what you're looking for here! Whether you're an experienced colorist or a beginner, whether you want to calm your mind or unleash your creativity, whether you just want to color or go crazy with crafting, this book has you covered, and here's why!

Need some advice? No problem! If you're a beginner, you'll learn everything you need to know to get started, from supplies to colorful inspiration. If you'd like a little help, we've provided guided coloring pages in the center of the book that start you off with a suggested color palette, finished example, and encouraging words. There's no need to feel intimidated!

Feeling creative? If you're looking for something new, check out our patterning and coloring techniques. Learn all about tangling and pumping up your pages with shading and blending. If you're feeling crafty, take a look at our ideas for craft projects incorporating colored pages.

Need to unwind? We get it! Every single page in this book was developed and hand-drawn by the author to give you the maximum benefits possible from coloring the images. By working with these designs, we know you are going to become relaxed, energized, and focused!

We know this book is going to give you exactly what you need: a little relaxation, some crafty ideas, and loads of coloring. What are you waiting for? It's time to get started!

MEET ARROLYNN

A Florida native, Arrolynn Weiderhold received a B.F.A. in Illustration from Ringling College of Art and Design and currently resides in Washington D.C., where she spends her time sketching at the zoo, museums, parks, and cafés. She draws inspiration from her collections of children's books, greeting cards, fabrics, and anything else she can get her hands on.

Frame your designs
for beautiful home accents.

ISBN 978-1-4972-0232-0

This edition created especially for Michaels Stores by New Design Originals, an imprint of Fox Chapel Publishing.

Fox Chapel focuses on providing real value to our customers through the printing and book production process. We strive to select quality paper that is also eco-friendly. This book is printed on archival-quality, acid-free paper that can be expected to last for at least 200 years. It meets the minimum requirements of the American National Standard for Information Sciences—Permanence of Paper for Printed Library Materials, ANSI/NISO Z39.48-1992. This book is printed on paper produced from trees harvested from well-managed forests where measures are taken to protect wildlife, plants, and water quality.

Fair trade principles should also be recognized when dealing with the creative and artistic community. We are pleased that our business practices and payments to authors meet the criteria to display **DO Magazine's Fair Trade Seal of Approval**. In order to earn the seal, all of the artwork must be original (not clip art or public domain material); the author must be paid on a royalty basis at fair trade rates (not piecemeal or via flat rates), meaning the author participates financially in the success of his or her titles; and the work of contributing artists must be acknowledged in print. DO Magazine: Color, Tangle, Craft, Doodle, www.domagazines.com.

Printed in the United States of America
First printing

Cover art colored by Llara Pazdan. Back cover art colored by Annie Jump.
Craft projects and guided pages colored by Razell Alcazar (p. 3 coaster, p. 8 bottom, p. 79), Laura Brumby (p. 9 lower right), Nadena Gibson (p. 9 upper left, p. 65), Annie Jump (p. 8 top, p. 77), Lynette Parmenter (p. 3 journal, p. 69), Llara Pazdan (p. 9 lower left, p. 67), Rachel Simpson (p. 75), Darla Tjelmeland (p. 9 top right), Arrolynn Weiderhold (p. 2, p. 3 bag, p. 5 journal, p. 9 middle left, p. 71, p. 73).

The Benefits of Coloring

A quick Internet search on this topic will yield pages of articles with statistics and opinions from the scientific research and art therapy communities. If you want to learn all about the science behind the benefits of coloring, we recommend you check them out. In the meantime, here are some of our favorite reasons for picking up the colored pencils.

Coloring allows for personal and creative expression. When it comes to coloring and creativity, there is no right or wrong. It's all about expressing your creativity your way. There are no limits to what you can do and no judgment (you don't have to show your coloring to someone else if you don't want to). The creativity of coloring provides a break from daily routine and can even make us more creative in other areas of our lives, like at work.

Colored designs can be decoupaged onto countless surfaces to make unique home dec pieces, like these coasters.

Coloring allows us to unplug.
Coloring is totally screen free. It's just us, our supplies, and our creativity. Unplugging every once in a while is a great way to relax, focus, and recharge, so unplugging by coloring is doubly effective!

Coloring reduces stress and anxiety. Why? It's easy and therefore stress free. Even better, research shows that coloring actually relaxes the fear center of the brain, reducing stress and anxiety in the present, and improving the way we respond to stressful situations in the future!

Coloring brings about a meditative state.
Coloring requires some focus, but not extreme concentration. By occupying part of the brain with the simple, repetitive act of coloring, the rest of the mind is free to let go and relax, switch off other thoughts, and focus on the present moment.

Coloring connects both sides of your brain.
Coloring requires the logical, analytical side of your brain when choosing where colors go and filling in spaces in a design. It requires the imaginative side of your brain when selecting a color palette and making creative choices about patterning, shading, and blending. Doing these things together strengthens the connection between your right brain and left brain and also exercises your fine motor skills and vision.

Use your finished pieces to add a personal touch to cards, journals, and scrapbooks.

Transfer your colored designs onto fabric for custom bags, shirts, and more!

Coloring Supplies

As adult coloring grows in popularity, so has the variety of coloring supplies available. So, how do you choose? For coloring (and art in general), experimentation is the name of the game. What works well and feels comfortable for someone else might not work for you. When starting out, try a little bit of everything to get a feel for what you like and refine your choices from there. And remember, coloring is supposed to be fun and stress free. Don't get hung up on using the "right" marker. If you want some guidance, here are some things to consider when choosing coloring supplies.

Markers

If you like bright, saturated colors and quick results, you'll probably be drawn to markers. Markers yield vibrant colors and can cover a lot of ground quickly. For coloring, tip shape is an important consideration. Lots of adult coloring pages are intricate and have many small spaces. You want markers with points that will allow you to get into those tiny areas with precision. Markers with brush tips are very versatile, allowing you to color large spaces quickly while still being able to fill in small spaces. Even better, some markers are dual ended, with a brush tip at one end and a fine point at the other. Markers with bullet or chisel tips will make precision work tricky, but you can pair them with fine-tip pens in the same color—use the markers for large areas and the corresponding pens for detail work.

When it comes to markers, you will hear a lot of talk about alcohol- vs. water-based options. This refers to the contents of the marker—dye mixed with water or dye mixed with alcohol. If you're just getting started, you might be drawn to the more budget-friendly, water-based markers. As you grow more serious about coloring, you might be drawn to alcohol-based markers, which are built to last, often refillable, and are less prone to streaking, but they also come with a high price tag.

One great thing about professional-grade markers is that they are usually available for purchase individually. To experiment, try purchasing an inexpensive set of brush markers and one or two professional water-based and alcohol-based options. See which ones you like working with the most.

Colored Pencils

If you love adding depth and dimension to a colored design with shading and blending, colored pencils are the perfect fit for you. While high-quality markers *can* be layered and blended, colored pencils were *made* for this.

When purchasing colored pencils, point strength is an important consideration. This refers to how hard or soft the pigment within the pencil is. If you want to do lots of layering and blending, you'll appreciate pencils with soft point strength. These will provide a creamy application and cover large areas easily, but they will not hold a sharp point for long, so you'll have to do a fair amount of sharpening for detail work. If you want pencils that will get into all of the tiny spaces on your coloring page, you'll like pencils with hard point strength. These will stay sharper longer, giving you the best precision, but they will be more difficult to blend.

As you grow more serious about coloring, you might be looking for ways to create unique effects. Watercolor pencils give your piece a painted watercolor look without the need for painting expertise. You apply color with the pencils and then add water to create the painted effect. If you just want to color, though, regular colored pencils are all you need.

Like markers, colored pencils come at a variety of price points. To experiment, try purchasing an inexpensive student-grade set along with a few individual options at a higher price point. Purchase a variety of point strengths—soft, medium, and hard—to determine your preference.

Pens

If you love adding special touches to your coloring, pens are for you. With their fine points, regular colored pens can be used to color tiny spaces that your markers cannot get into, while paint pens and gel pens can be used to add patterning and accents on top of a piece that's already been colored.

If you really enjoy patterning, try purchasing one or two felt-tip pens to add doodles and details to a coloring page. You can pattern a design before coloring, or add the patterning to open areas like the background after coloring.

For special effects and accents, gel pens and paint pens are the way to go. Because their ink is opaque, these pens can be used to accent areas on pieces already colored with markers or colored pencils. Beyond that, you can purchase gel pens and paint pens in endless varieties, including metallic, sparkle, and neon, even glow in the dark! If you're not sure about the power of pens, purchase a white gel pen or paint pen and try using it to add accents to a colored design. We're sure you'll be back at the craft store looking for more!

Coloring Techniques

There are so many cool things you can do with a coloring page besides coloring it. You can make the design your own by adding patterning and flourishes, or you can add depth and dimension through shading and blending. Here are some techniques to try.

Patterning

Patterning might sound intimidating, but a pattern is really just a combination of basic shapes (like circles, lines, and triangles) that is repeated. And we can all draw triangles and circles, right? So we can definitely draw patterns. Here are some simple patterns for you to try.

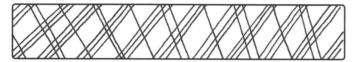

Lines. It doesn't get any easier! Draw them with even spacing, close together, far apart, or all three! Try drawing curved lines or lines that crisscross.

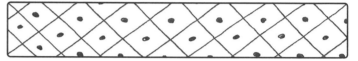

Checkerboard. Fill a space with a grid. Add something to alternating (or all) boxes in the grid—fill them in completely, add dots, add stripes, add hearts. Vary the spacing of the lines in your grid or try drawing it with wavy lines.

Circles. Draw them open or fill them in as dots. Make them all the same size or make some big and some small (like bubbles). Draw them in orderly rows or overlap them like ripples.

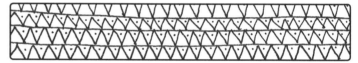

Triangles. Try adding triangles along a line on your coloring page. This is a really cool effect in and of itself, but you can take it further by adding dots or lines between the triangles or overlapping the triangles.

Need some help?

The Zentangle® method is a meditative drawing technique that uses simple, step-by-step patterns called tangles to produce unique art pieces. There are hundreds of tangles available online, a perfect resource for pattern ideas or step-by-step instructions. Try one of the tangles below on your next coloring page. To learn more about the Zentangle method, check out *Joy of Zentangle* or *Zentangle Basics, Expanded Workbook Edition* or connect with a Certified Zentangle Teacher (CZT) in your area (*www.zentangle.com*).

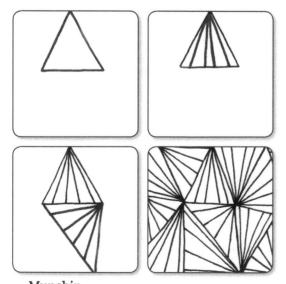

Munchin
An original Zentangle design

Flying Geese
Tangle by Suzanne McNeill, CZT

Shading and Blending

Shading and blending are wonderful ways to make a coloring page look more realistic, and they don't require a lot of expertise. Shading uses tints and shades of one color to add dimension. Blending uses multiple colors together to create cool gradations. Here are some simple ways to use shading and blending to make a design jump right off the page.

Go around the edges. Shading around the edge of a shape will add dimension. This can be done around a large shape, or around smaller areas within a shape. For example, you could shade around the entire flower (left) or just around the center circle (right).

Work from end to end. Try giving a shape dimension by working from a dark shade at one end to a light shade at the other end. The leaf at right is colored with three shades of green. To re-create this effect, select three shades of the same color: light, medium, and dark. Color the entire shape with the light color. Then, starting at one end, color two-thirds of the shape with the medium color. Then, starting at the same end, color one-third of the shape with the dark color. Go over the entire shape with the light color to help smooth the transitions between the shades.

Work from inside out or outside in. The same technique used to shade a shape from end to end can be used to shade a shape from the inside out (left) or the outside in (right).

Blend instead of shade. Blending follows the same steps as shading except it uses multiple colors instead of tints and shades of one color. For blending, you'll want a starting color, one or two transition colors, and a finishing color. For example, to blend from yellow to red, you'll want yellow (starting color), light orange (transition color), dark orange (transition color), and red (finishing color). Since you're working with four colors, mentally divide the shape you're working on into quarters. Color the entire shape yellow. Starting at one end, color three-quarters of the shape light orange. Starting at the same end, color half of the shape dark orange. Starting at the same end, color one-quarter of the shape red. Go over the entire shape with yellow to smooth over the transitions.

Gallery Wall

What better way to display your colored designs than by transforming them into a gallery wall feature! Here are some tips and tricks for creating a stunning gallery wall.

Map it out. How many frames do you want and in what size? Do you want an orderly grid pattern or a creative, eclectic layout? Will your frames be the same size, or will you enlarge or shrink some of your designs to fit frames of different sizes? Try out your design by cutting different frame sizes out of newspaper and hanging them on your wall to see if you like the look.

Pick your designs. Will you use only coloring pages or include some other pieces? What do you want to feature: your favorite designs, designs that are thematically similar, or designs with complementary color palettes?

Craft it up. If you're feeling extra crafty, try transferring one of your designs to wood or canvas. Experiment with color mats, or try cutting out small designs and attaching them to colorful paper for a pop of color in the background.

Pick your frames. Will all of your frames be exactly the same, or perhaps different styles but all in the same color? Maybe you want to mix and match black and white or choose bright, modern colors. Do you want frames with or without mats or a mix of both?

Hang it up. When all of your pieces are crafted and framed, it's time to hang them up using your chosen layout!

A Personal Touch

Coloring pages are a great way to add a personal touch to your home, your crafts, and even your gift giving. Check out the reverse side of each coloring page for a space designed for your creativity. Use it as a journaling page or a place to record notes about your coloring mediums and techniques. The page is made to be folded in three so you can mail your coloring page with a personal note if you're giving it as a gift.

Color by Ninna Hellman. *Colored pencils, markers*

© Arrolynn Weiderhold and Design Originals

THE EARTH Laughs IN FLOWERS

—RALPH WALDO EMERSON

Color by Annie Jump. *Colored pencils*

Color by Dawn Collins. *Colored pencils*

Color by Arrolynn Weiderhold. *Colored pencils*

Color by Darla Tjelmeland. *Colored pencils, markers*

Color by Razell Alcazar. *Colored pencils, brush pens, gel pens*

There is always music amongst the trees in the garden, but our hearts must be very quiet to hear it.

—Minnie Aumonier

Date

Name

Let us dance in the sun,
wearing wild flowers in our hair...

—Susan Polis Schutz

Date

Name

My soul is in the sky.

—William Shakespeare, *A Midsummer Night's Dream*

Date   Name

Where flowers bloom, so does hope.

—Lady Bird Johnson

Date

Name

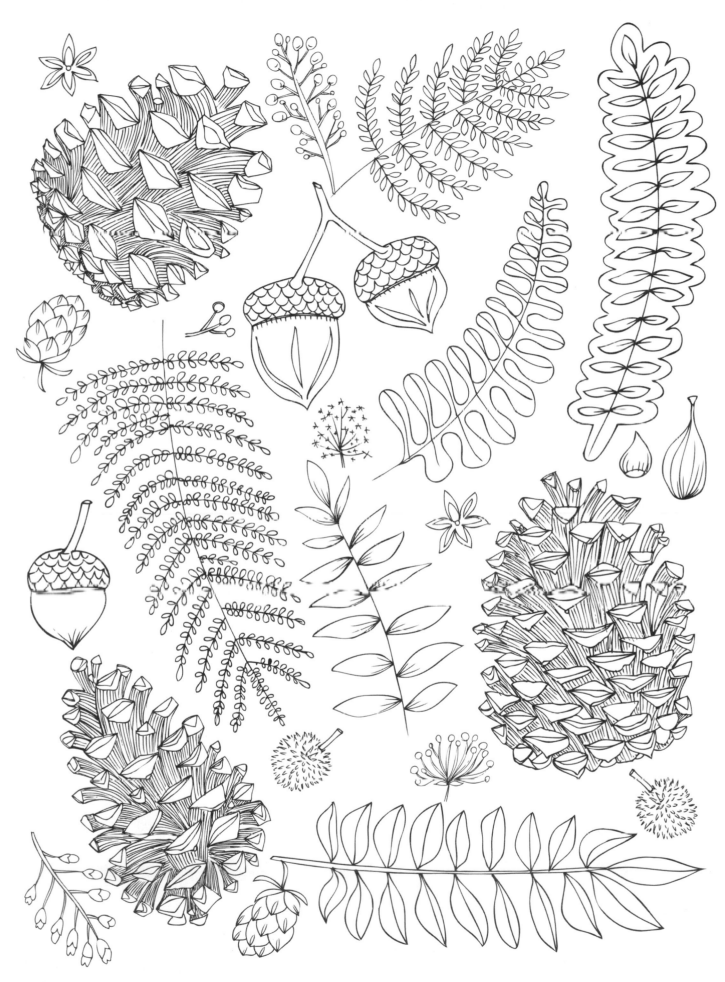

The tallest oak in the forest was once just
a little nut that held its ground.

—Unknown

_____
_____
_____
_____
_____
_____
_____
_____
_____
_____
_____

Date   Name

Be Silly, BE HONEST, BE KIND.

-RALPH WALDO EMERSON

We're all golden sunflowers inside.

—Allen Ginsberg

Date   Name

Raise your words, not your voice.
It is rain that grows flowers, not thunder.

—Rumi

_____

_____

_____

_____

_____

_____

_____

_____

_____

_____

_____

Date   Name

Flowers can't solve all problems
but they're a great start.

—Unknown

Date

Name

Every flower must grow through dirt.

—Laurie Jean Sennott

_____

_____

_____

_____

_____

_____

_____

_____

_____

_____

_____

Date   Name

Those who dwell among the beauties and mysteries
of the earth are never alone or weary of life.

—Rachel Carson

Date   Name

Be patient with yourself.
Nothing in nature blooms all year.

—Unknown

_____

_____

_____

_____

_____

_____

_____

_____

_____

_____

_____

Date   Name

Sometimes when you're in a dark place, you think
you've been buried, but you've actually been planted.

—Christine Caine

Date

Name

May you always hear the whisper of wings.

—Unknown

_____
_____
_____
_____
_____
_____
_____
_____
_____
_____

Date   Name

To plant a garden is to believe in tomorrow.

—Audrey Hepburn

_____

_____

_____

_____

_____

_____

_____

_____

_____

_____

_____

_____

_____

Date   Name

Wherever life plants you, bloom with grace.

—French proverb

Date   Name

Don't try to rush things that need time to grow.

—Unknown

Date

Name

I'd rather wear flowers in my hair than diamonds around my neck.

—Emma Goldman

_____

_____

_____

_____

_____

_____

_____

_____

_____

_____

_____

Date   Name

May your search through Nature lead you to yourself.

—Unknown

Date   Name

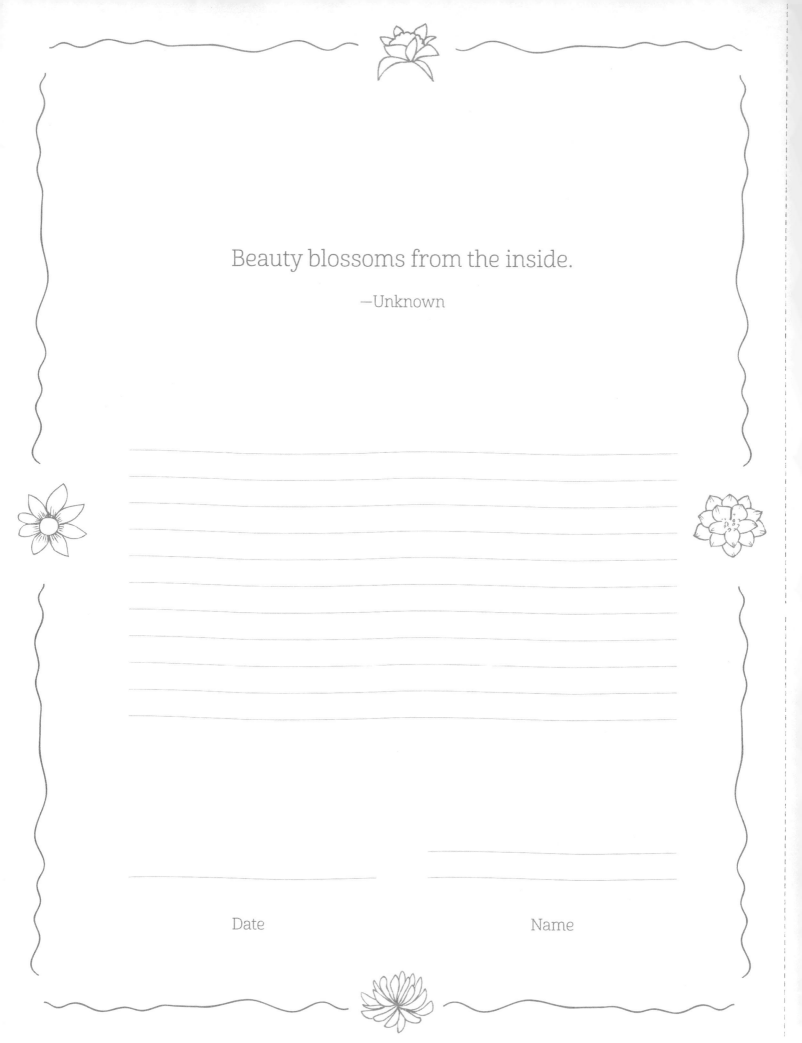

Beauty blossoms from the inside.

—Unknown

Date   Name

I'm planting a tree to teach me to gather strength
from my deepest roots.

—Andrea Koehle Jones, *The Wish Trees*

_____

_____

_____

_____

_____

_____

_____

_____

_____

_____

_____

Date   Name

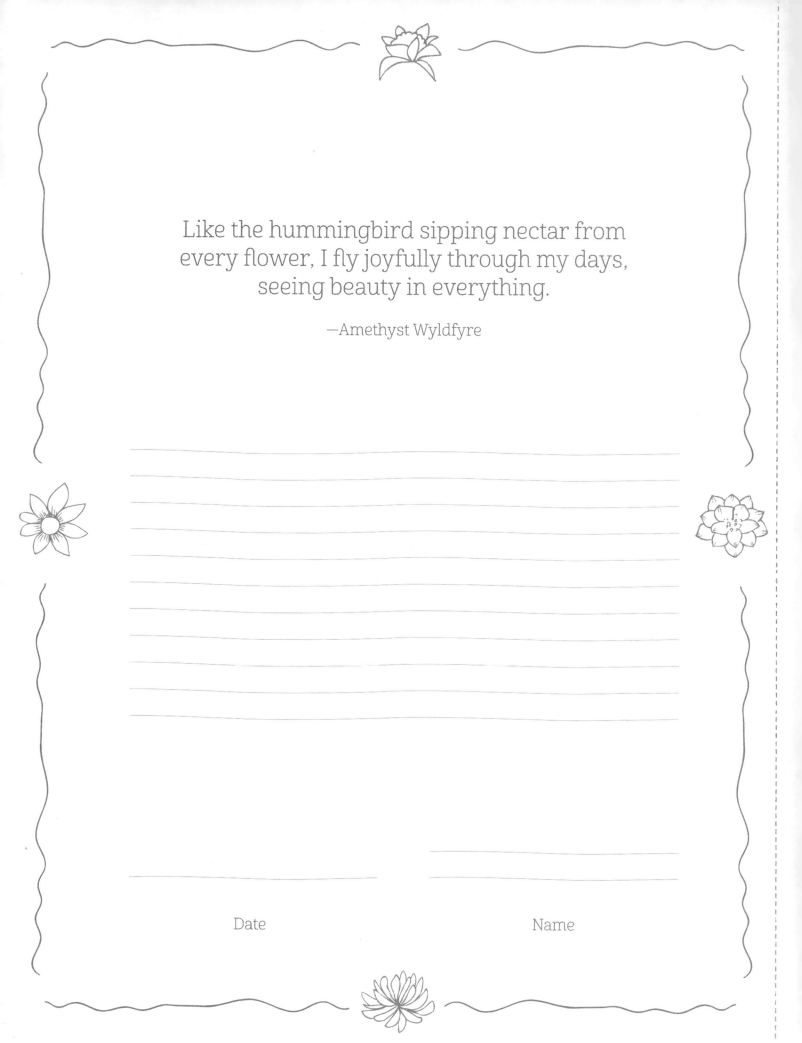

Like the hummingbird sipping nectar from
every flower, I fly joyfully through my days,
seeing beauty in everything.

—Amethyst Wyldfyre

Date   Name

Flowers are the music of the ground,
from earth's lips spoken without a sound.

—Edwin Curran

Date   Name

I must have flowers, always, and always.

—Claude Monet

Date   Name

If flowers can teach themselves to bloom
after winter passes, so can you.

—Noor Shirazie

_____

Date   Name

These cute little succulents look great in bright, warm colors like pink and orange with pops of cool colors like green, blue, and purple for contrast.

Good things take time.

—Unknown

Designs that incorporate complementary colors (like yellow and purple) will really pop. A bit of light research into color theory will help you gain confidence selecting colors.

Like wildflowers, you must allow yourself to grow in all the places people never thought you would.

—Unknown

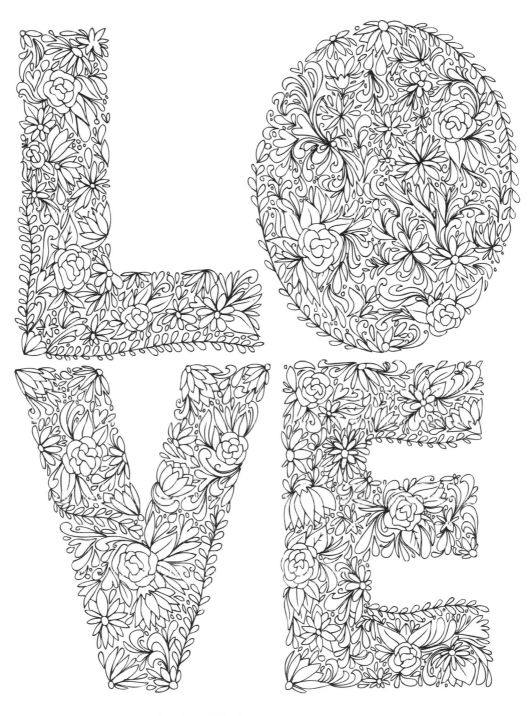

© Arrolynn Weiderhold and Design Originals

The separate letters in this design provide an opportunity
to try a different set of colors in each one.

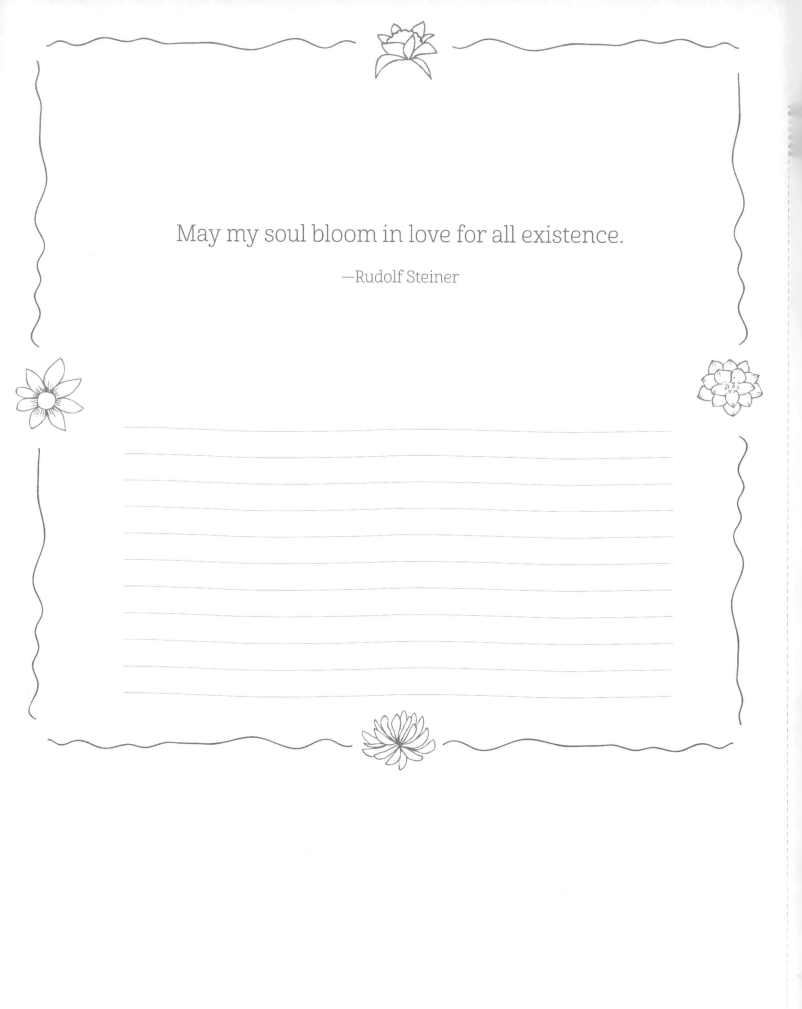

May my soul bloom in love for all existence.

—Rudolf Steiner

Soft, pastel shades create a beautiful springtime palette. Use more vibrant colors to give the same design a summery feel.

Happiness held is the seed; happiness
shared is the flower.

—John Harrigan

© Arrolynn Weiderhold and Design Originals

Mixing warm and cool colors is a great way to make sure the
different shapes on a coloring page stand out from one another.

We are all different flowers from the same garden.

—Unknown

THE EARTH
Laughs
IN
FLOWERS

-RALPH WALDO EMERSON

Try a color scheme with analogous colors (like red, orange, and yellow) with some complementary colors (like green and blue) added in for contrast.

I want to feel as free as the flowers.

—Unknown

_____

_____

_____

_____

_____

_____

_____

_____

_____

_____

_____

© Arrolynn Weiderhold and Design Originals

You don't need hundreds of colors to create a beautiful design. This piece is transformed with just a few hues and the use of shading.

Leave room in your garden for the fairies to dance.

—Unknown

© Arrolynn Weiderhold and Design Originals

Use a dark color for your background and light, bright colors for all of the other elements. They will really pop off the page!

May all your weeds be wildflowers.

—Unknown

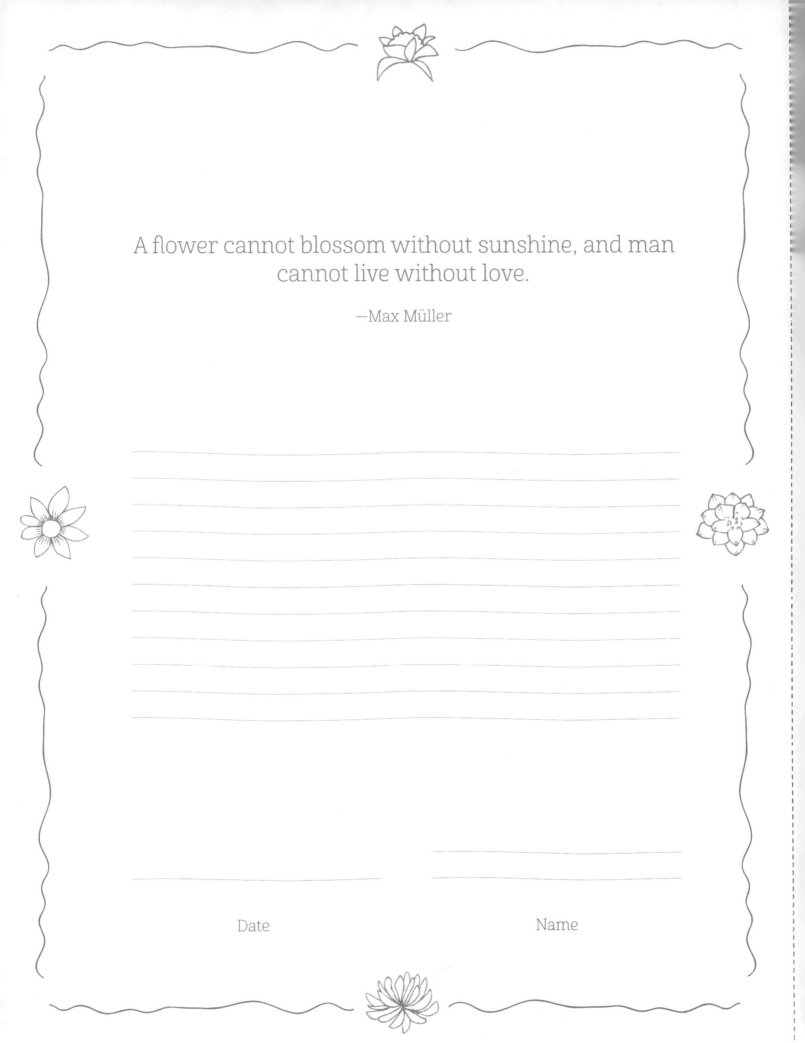

A flower cannot blossom without sunshine, and man
cannot live without love.

—Max Müller

_____

_____

_____

_____

_____

_____

_____

_____

_____

_____

Date   Name

Plant seeds of kindness. Harvest a garden of love.

—Unknown

_____

_____

_____

_____

_____

_____

_____

_____

_____

_____

_____

_____

Date   Name

Think of all the beauty still left around
you and be happy.

—Anne Frank

Date   Name

The flower doesn't dream of the bee.
It blossoms and the bee comes.

—Unknown

Date

Name

There came a time when the risk
to remain tight in the bud was more painful
than the risk it took to blossom.

—Anaïs Nin

Date   Name

In any given moment we have two options: to step forward into growth or to step back into safety.

—Abraham Maslow

Date   Name

There are always flowers for those who
want to see them.

—Henri Matisse

_____
_____
_____
_____
_____
_____
_____
_____
_____
_____

Date   Name

Everything grows better with love.

—Unknown

_____

_____

_____

_____

_____

_____

_____

_____

_____

_____

_____   _____

Date   Name

A beautiful life will bloom from a beautiful mind that is nurtured by beautiful thoughts. At any time you can allow beauty to flow within you.

—Dodinsky

Date

Name

Be not afraid of growing slowly,
be afraid only of standing still.

—Chinese proverb

Date   Name

the BEST THINGS in Life ARE FREE

Some old-fashioned things like fresh air and sunshine are hard to beat.

—Laura Ingalls Wilder

Date

Name

A flower blossoms for its own joy.

—Oscar Wilde

Date   Name

The flower that blooms in adversity is the most rare
and beautiful of all.

—Mulan

_____

_____

_____

_____

_____

_____

_____

_____

_____

_____

Date   Name

You are built, not to shrink down to less, but to blossom into more.

—Oprah Winfrey

_____

_____

_____

_____

_____

_____

_____

_____

_____

_____

_____

Date   Name

Let the waters settle and you will see the moon and
the stars mirrored in your own being.

—Rumi

Date

Name

Don't hurry. Don't worry. And be sure to smell the
flowers along the way.

—Walter Hagen

_____
_____
_____
_____
_____
_____
_____
_____
_____
_____

Date   Name

Don't go through life, grow through life.

—Eric Butterworth

_____

_____

_____

_____

_____

_____

_____

_____

_____

_____

_____

                                    _____

_____   _____

Date   Name

Forget not that the earth delights to feel your bare feet and the winds long to play with your hair.

—Kahlil Gibran

Date   Name

Every flower is a soul blossoming in nature.

—Gérard de Nerval

Date

Name

Some birds are not meant to be caged, that's all.
Their feathers are too bright, their songs too
sweet and wild.

—Stephen King, *The Shawshank Redemption*

Date   Name

© Arrolynn Weiderhold and Design Originals

If you look the right way, you can see that the whole world is a garden.

—Frances Hodgson Burnett, *The Secret Garden*

Date

Name

Great things are done by a series of small things
brought together.

—Vincent van Gogh

_____
_____
_____
_____
_____
_____
_____
_____
_____
_____

Date   Name

Deep in their roots all flowers keep the light.

—Theodore Roethke

_____

_____

_____

_____

_____

_____

_____

_____

_____

_____

_____

Date   Name

All the flowers of all the tomorrows
are in the seeds of today.

—Indian proverb

Date   Name

And the secret garden bloomed and bloomed and every morning revealed new miracles.

—Frances Hodgson Burnett, *The Secret Garden*

Date   Name

I am in awe of flowers. Not because of their colors,
but because even though they have dirt in their roots,
they still grow. They still bloom.

—Unknown

_____

Date   Name

Kind hearts are the gardens, Kind thoughts
are the roots, Kind words are the flowers,
Kind deeds are the fruits. Take care of your garden
and keep out the weeds; Fill it with sunshine,
Kind words and Kind deeds.

—Henry Wadsworth Longfellow

Date   Name

There's nothing wrong with having a tree as a friend.

—Bob Ross

_____

_____

_____

_____

_____

_____

_____

_____

_____

_____

_____

Date   Name

Live life in full bloom.

—Unknown

_____

Date   Name

© Arrolynn Weiderhold and Design Originals

Your wings already exist. All you have to do is fly.

—Unknown

_____

_____

_____

_____

_____

_____

_____

_____

_____

_____

_____

Date   Name

Every experience makes you grow.

—Unknown

Date   Name

Let it grow, let it grow,
Let it blossom, let it flow.
In the sun, the rain, the snow,
Love is lovely, let it grow.

—Eric Clapton

Date

Name